CONTENTS

Preface —5
To the Reader —7
Introduction —9

1. Trouble in the New Testament Church —13
2. Difficulties in the Church Today —36
3. Other Causes of Confusion —74

Epilogue —82
For Further Reading and Study —85
The Author —87
Mennonite Faith Series —*Inside back cover*

Marian Hostetler

Some People Are Throwing You into Confusion

PIERRE WIDMER

Translated by Marian Hostetler

HERALD PRESS
Scottdale, Pennsylvania
Kitchener, Ontario

Bible quotations are from *The New International Version*, copyright © 1978 by The New York International Bible Society. Used by permission of Zondervan Publishing House.

SOME PEOPLE ARE THROWING YOU INTO CONFUSION
Originally published in French in 1982 under the title, *Il y a des gens qui vous troublent*, by Les Cahiers de Christ Seul, Montbéliard, France.
English translation copyright © 1984 by Mennonite Board of Missions, Elkhart, Ind. 46515. All rights reserved.
Published by Herald Press, Scottdale, Pa. 15683
Released simultaneously in Canada by Herald Press, Kitchener, Ont. N2G 4M5
Library of Congress Catalog Card Number: 83-82879
International Standard Book Number: 0-8361-3358-7
Printed in the United States of America
Design: Alice B. Shetler/Art by Elmore Byler

84 85 86 87 88 10 9 8 7 6 5 4 3 2 1

Distributed overseas by Mennonite Board of Missions, 1251 Virginia Avenue, Harrisonburg, Va. 22801-2497.

PREFACE

"A fighting book"—that's what I thought as I finished reading this manuscript. It is a cry, a prophecy, but it also reflects the convictions of a thinking man. And the life and ministry of its author is consistent with his writing. It is an impressive witness based on a deep desire to understand the Bible. The author brings from it well-balanced teachings and illuminates these by rich and varied experiences. He writes as one who has true loyalty and total commitment to the Scriptures.

The qualities that make us love (and sometimes fear) the author are found in this work. For myself, I'm appreciative. I appreciate the man, the warrior,

5

the prophet. I'm astonished at his contacts, at his knowledge of the "evangelical world," at his biblical knowledge. I agree with his adherence to the original values of the Mennonite movement, his faithfulness to the local congregation, his emphasis on living one's faith every day, and to his firm and upright faith.

But I must not prolong this—it is only a preface. Let the readers form their own opinions. We hope that those who read this book, including members of our congregations, will go from confusion to discernment, from discernment to combat (the contention for the faith that was entrusted to the saints according to Jude 3), from combat to calm, and from calm to firmness, because "no one can lay any foundation other than the one already laid, which is Jesus Christ" (1 Corinthians 3:11).

—Bernard Huck

TO THE READER

"Test everything. Hold on to the good" (1 Thessalonians 5:21).

This book may not please everyone, so we invite the reader to remember these words of the apostle Paul.

Our goal is not to please (see Galatians 1:10). It is to warn, to teach, to lead you to think, so that if you read this book with an open mind, you may be built up in the faith in Jesus Christ. If your mind is made up and closed, it will be difficult for you to see or to retain the good which may be found in these pages.

Many things confuse Christians in all the churches today, including our own. It has always been that way, more or less, throughout the history of the church. In the sixteenth century there was much confusion in the minds of people and in society itself. During the Reformation many long-held beliefs came into question. The Anabaptist movement brought still more customs and beliefs into question. At that time it was important to examine everything and then to keep what was good. This is true for today as well.

Don't expect to find here any information or reflection on the dangerous cults of our time which are growing everywhere. We want, rather, to speak about the troubles inside the churches and what causes them—the troubles which disturb the lives of Christians.

This booklet is a part of the Mennonite Faith Series listed inside the back cover. It originally appeared in the French language, and after translation, was adapted by the editors for easy reading and further translation into other languages. Anyone wanting to study the theme further may check the references listed in the back of the booklet.

INTRODUCTION

"Some people are throwing you into confusion" (Galatians 1:7).

Don't "become easily unsettled" (2 Thessalonians 2:2).

Each child of God, each disciple of Jesus Christ knows the word that the Savior gave to his disciples in the Upper Room during his last talk with them. John reports it in his Gospel (14:1, 27): "Do not let your hearts be troubled and do not be afraid."

Jesus mentioned several times in his teaching ministry the kind of attitude which is needed to live daily with God.

" 'Do not worry about your life.... Why do you

worry?... So do not worry.... Do not worry about your life.... Why do you worry?... Do not worry about it ...'" (Matthew 6:25, 28, 31; Luke 12:22, 26, 29).

No doubt these verses address the natural tendency of people to be too concerned with physical life—eating, drinking, clothing, shelter, and the conditions we live in. But Jesus' message also concerns the spiritual life, the life to come, the true life, eternal life.

Peace Is the Believer's Privilege

Although disciples of Jesus may face suffering, persecution, and death, their minds can know a deep feeling of peace:

"Peace I leave with you; my peace I give to you. I do not give to you as the world gives. Do not let your hearts be troubled and do not be afraid" (John 14:27). Note that these words were spoken as Jesus faced his own suffering and death. They were given to prepare the disciples for his crucifixion—the greatest difficulty they would have to experience; his words about leaving them were enough to trouble their hearts and minds continually. Their beloved Master was going to be taken from them under atrocious conditions: They would be alone, a flock scattered after their Good Shepherd had been struck down! (as it's written in Zechariah 13:7 and Matthew 26:31).

But Jesus wants his followers to have peace no matter what happens.

"But a time is coming, and has come, when you will be scattered, each to his own home. You will leave me all alone. Yet I am not alone, for my Father is with me. I have told you these things, so that in me you may have peace. In this world you will have trouble. But take heart! I have overcome the world. John 16:32, 33.

When they see him again in John 20 after his death and resurrection, the Lord Jesus restates his promise. He continues to repeat to his followers: "Peace be with you! Peace be with you!" (John 20:19, 21, 26).

Certainly the Lord Jesus himself experienced hours of unutterable anguish in the Garden of Gethsemane and on the cross of Calvary. Beforehand, in telling his friends about these dreadful moments of sacrifice to take away the sins of the world, Jesus had prayed to the Father:

> Now my heart is troubled, and what shall I say? "Father, save me from this hour?" No, it was for this very reason I came to this hour. Father, glorify your name! John 12:27, 28.

This is the deep mystery of the atonement, of the abandoning of the Son by the Father, of the profound depth of the trouble in our beloved Savior at the time of his sacrifice.

"My God, my God, why have you forsaken me?" he cried, accomplishing perfectly the prophecy of Psalm 22:2 (Matthew 27:46; Mark 15:34). He died so that we, redeemed sinners, united to Christ, shall never more be forsaken (Matthew 28:20).

So why is it that so many Christians, young and old, already in the time of the early church, were so "confused" in their faith? Why? They have no peace, and it's not because of persecutions, or because they don't believe in the Lord Jesus, or because they do not believe enough! We must mention that where persecution arises, this type of "confusion" does not arise. It is rather where one enjoys outward peace, many material benefits, and an easy life that Christians are inwardly troubled instead of being filled with "the peace of God, which transcends all understanding" (Philippians 4:7).

Why is this? Something has entered the picture which we must have the courage to face. One day Jesus, explaining a parable, said: "An enemy had done that."

Today we must say to many Christians as Paul wrote to the Galatians: "Some people are throwing you into confusion!"

1

TROUBLE IN THE NEW TESTAMENT CHURCH

BEFORE discussing the present situation in the churches, especially in the evangelical ones, we will see what happened in the "apostolic" church. It is known by this name because it was founded by the Lord's apostles themselves. Under the power of the Holy Spirit, they went everywhere preaching the word of God, the good news of salvation, the message of repentance and faith in God. As people responded to this good news, the church took root and grew.

It is in these first churches that we also find the first instances of "those who confuse" the believers and the Christian communities.

The Antioch Example

"We have heard that some went out from us without our authorization and disturbed you, troubling your minds by what they said" (Acts 15:24).

Acts 13, 14 report briefly the first missionary journey of Paul and Barnabas and their return to the church that had sent them. This was according to the Holy Spirit's direction after the church of Antioch fasted, prayed, and laid hands on them.

A beautiful church, this church of Antioch! I don't speak of a building—buildings aren't mentioned in the Bible! But I speak of a church founded by the witness of people from Cyprus and Cyrene, people who fled from there because of the first persecution of the believers (Acts 8:1-4 and 11:19). They preached the good news—not only to the Jews, but also to Greeks.

"The Lord's hand was with them, and a great number of people believed and turned to the Lord" (Acts 11:21).

The news of this spread to Jerusalem (Acts 11:22) and the church there decided to send Barnabas to Antioch.

> When he arrived and saw the evidence of the grace of God, he was glad and encouraged them all to remain true to the Lord with all their hearts. He was a good man, full of the Holy Spirit and faith, and a great number of people were brought to the Lord. Acts 11:23, 24.

Barnabas was a "good man." (Not everyone is good, even though they may have an important function in the church!) He exhorted them to remain faithful to the Lord Jesus, who showed "the grace of God" and secured salvation for the repentant sinner. These are the basics of Christian faith and life.

So Barnabas was teaching at Antioch and building up the believers in their faith in Christ. He was helping to complete the brave witness of those Christians who had been scattered by persecution and who had come as far as Antioch from Cyprus and Cyrene. But Barnabas was not satisfied. He went to Tarsus "to look for Saul" (Acts 11:25). Barnabas had previously been used by God to introduce Saul of Tarsus to the group of apostles (Acts 9:26-30).

So then Paul is with Barnabas at Antioch (Acts 11:26), for "when he found him, he brought him to Antioch. So for a whole year Barnabas and Saul met with the church and taught great numbers of people. The disciples were first called Christians at Antioch."

"Christians" was probably at first a nickname for these followers of Christ. We know many other groups over the centuries were named after a servant of God who had taught and led them to become better disciples of Jesus; we ourselves have the name "Mennonite" from an early leader, Menno Simons.

Antioch was indeed a privileged church, having been founded and built up in Christ. It was also the first church to "provide help for the brothers living in Judea" during a famine. Announced by the prophet Agabus, it took place during the reign of the Emperor Claudius (Acts 11:27-30).

Yet this church at Antioch, which had everything going for it, would soon be "confused." Paul and

Barnabas had just returned from their first missionary journey and reported "all that God had done through them" when the testing began (Acts 14:26-28). Acts 15:1 says,

> Some men came down from Judea to Antioch and were teaching the brothers: "Unless you are circumcised according to the custom taught by Moses, you cannot be saved."

For these men the gospel of Jesus Christ was not enough. One must also be circumcised according to the law of Moses. Thus, they brought to this united, living, faithful church legalism and the following of rituals. "Dispute and debate" destroyed their peace (Acts 15:2). Therefore, the church sent a delegation to Jerusalem where the problem could be studied and solved with the help of God's Word and the Holy Spirit in the congregation. This Jerusalem Conference with the apostles and elders is reported in some detail in Acts 15:4-29. At the close of this meeting, a letter was written in the name of the apostles and elders to explain the agreement of the entire church at Jerusalem (Acts 15:22). It reminds the Christians who were at Antioch, Syria, and Cilicia:

> We have heard that some went out from us without our authorization and disturbed you, troubling your minds by what they said. Acts 15:24.

This brotherly letter, short and moderate, avoids vain and emotional discussions. It gives simple instructions and practical advice regarding the customs of that time. It rejected legalism and ritual, which some wished to impose on believers. *It affirmed that salvation is only through Christ's sacrifice.* I have always admired the remarkable fairness and the calm assurance of the authors of this letter.

> "It seemed good to the Holy Spirit and to us not to burden you with anything beyond the following requirements: You are to abstain from food sacrificed to idols, from blood, from the meat of strangled animals and from sexual immorality. You will do well to avoid these things." Acts 15:28, 29.

What marvelous liberty the children of God have! Such a message from Jerusalem must have delighted and encouraged the Antioch Christians, bringing peace to their hearts and relationships.

This was the first attack of legalism and ritualism on the early church—saying that a Christian needed to follow all the customs and rites of the Jewish law to be truly saved.

But this attack, which troubled the Antioch Christians and disturbed their souls, was not the only one.

The Galatia Example

The letter of Paul to the Galatians follows the incident at Antioch. It was written to bring peace to the Galatian believers. Their spirits were troubled by a teaching which says that faith in Jesus Christ for salvation is not enough.

Acts 16 reports the beginning of Paul's second missionary journey with Silas and Timothy as his companions. Their preaching in Galatia is briefly mentioned in verse 6, along with their work in Phrygia, a neighboring province in Asia Minor. Paul traveled through Galatia and Phrygia again during his third missionary journey. We may be sure that the Galatians were well taught in the Christian faith, because Paul at that time strengthened "all the disciples" (Acts 18:23).

But here again something happened. The text does not explain the exact origin of this attack against the gospel, as taught by Paul. But apparently the Galatian Christians were deeply troubled in their faith and in their conduct by several persons known by their goal: "Some people are throwing you into confusion and are trying to pervert the gospel of Christ" (Galatians 1:7).

Some teachers were tearing down the faith of the Galatian Christians and trying to turn them away from the gospel of Jesus Christ. This was happening in the church, among the community of believers. Those who had been firmly attached to the Lord Jesus and to the good news of salvation by faith in his saving work were quickly deserting Christ (Galatians 1:6).

The apostle Paul fought vigorously against such enemies, these spreaders of another gospel. His letter to the Galatians contends for "the faith that was once for all entrusted to the saints" (Jude 3).

The letter's central theme is Christian liberty—freedom from sin and from the law of sin to live according to the Spirit. Sinful nature has been condemned by Jesus Christ's death on the cross for the forgiveness of our sins. *By the Holy Spirit given to us, we now live in fellowship with the risen Lord Jesus.* There is absolutely nothing which can be added to this perfect work of salvation. The Christian is under no obligation to practice the rite of circumcision, which is the sign of the old covenant. Paul ends his letter by writing:

> May I never boast except in the cross of our Lord Jesus Christ, through which the world has been crucified to me, and I to the world. Neither circumcision nor uncircumcision means anything; what counts is a new creation. Galatians 6:14, 15.

Already in Galatians 5:6 he affirms categorically:

> For in Christ Jesus neither circumcision nor uncircumcision has any value. The only thing that counts is faith expressing itself through love.

Paul is severe with those who had thus upset the churches of Galatia. He writes, "The one who is throwing you into confusion will pay the penalty, whoever he may be" (Galatians 5:10). And again, "As for those agitators, I wish they would go the whole way and emasculate themselves!" (Galatians 5:12).

Paul's harsh words show the wickedness of any action or teaching which claims to add to the gospel. His words reveal the fearful weight borne by those who pull down the church under the pretense of a superior revelation.

The Thessalonica Example

In the second letter to the Thessalonians, Paul's principal theme is Christ's return, his second coming.

> Concerning the coming of our Lord Jesus Christ and our being gathered to him, we ask you, brothers, not to become easily unsettled or alarmed by some

> prophecy, report or letter supposed to have come from us, saying that the day of the Lord has already come. 2 Thessalonians 2:1, 2.

This report or letter deeply troubled the hearts and minds of the believers—they no longer knew what to think regarding Christ's return. Although Paul was accused of originating this deceptive report, he challenges the accusation (2:1-12). The fact is clear: the church at Thessalonica was troubled by Christian preachers who were manipulating them under seemingly the best of motives—"to be taken up with the Lord!"

The motive is excellent, the concern is right: not to let oneself be surprised by the coming of Christ but to be ready for his return.

What is not good and not right is to become so excited about this as to lose one's direction. To be "deceived" is the word Paul uses. "Don't let anyone deceive you in any way" (2 Thessalonians 2:3). He adds other precise warnings concerning "the man of lawlessness," "the man doomed to destruction," the lawless one who precedes the coming of the Lord with "every sort of evil that deceives" (2 Thessalonians 2:3-12).

The Lord Jesus himself often cautioned his disciples *to be on their guard against the danger of deception.* His prophetic speeches reported in Matthew 24, Mark 13, and Luke 17 and 21 underline this. But it seems that the Christians of Thessalonica had forgotten this and let themselves be "easily unsettled" by these preachers, agents of deception. Their message troubled the hearers instead of building the believers up in peace. Instead of helping believers to grow spiritually and to wait in faithful obedience for the return of Jesus, these deceivers caused uncertainty and thereby hindered growth.

The return of Christ is a favorite subject for those who would sow trouble among Christians. So-called "inspired" speculations about "end times" brought trouble to the Thessalonians. Such groundless affirmations have troubled Christians throughout the centuries and continue to disturb Christians even now.

Conclusion: It is certain that Paul in his oral and written teaching had left a place for the possibility of a near return of the Lord. Read, for example, 1 Thessalonians 2:19; 3:13; 4:15-17; 5:4, not to mention his other epistles. The Thessalonians, under the influence of a sick or wild imagination, considered their own thoughts to be prophecies of the Spirit. Thus, they thought themselves already in the period when the Lord had returned. They did not see that this contradicted the teaching of Jesus himself. They were confused in both what to think and how to live. This is no doubt one of the most serious cases of confusion in spirit and heart during the history of the church. "Don't become easily unsettled or alarmed" was the necessary conclusion then. It also is today.

Warnings to the Romans

In this epistle the apostle Paul doesn't use the same expressions as we have noted in the previous examples. But several times he warns his readers against allowing various influences to create disorder in their Christian life and thought.

According to Romans 3:8 and 6:1, 15, some teachers are teaching moral and doctrinal looseness.

They thought, since grace abounds where sin abounds and since God is love and wants to save all people, then let's do evil so that good may result (Romans 3:8). Let us live in sin so that God's forgiveness and grace may abound so much more (Romans 6:1). Let us sin, since we are no longer under the law but under grace (Romans 6:15).

Such is the teaching, supposedly Christian, that troubled many believers in the first century and still troubles many today. Since Jesus Christ gave his life as a ransom to pay for and to take away the sin of the world, why be so concerned about sin?

However, Romans 6 to 8 were written to refute such blasphemous teachings and to encourage Christians to live holy, Spirit-led lives. Paul expects us to triumph over the impulses of "the flesh" (that is, over our nature, which is sinful and tends toward doing evil).

When this truth is not kept clear, trouble and disquiet arise in the spirits of individual Christians and in their communities. We can expect confusion if we forget that justification by faith calls for a life made holy by Christ and the Holy Spirit, dedicated to God!

Paul returned to this theme often in his epistles, each of which contains a doctrinal and an ethical part. The ethical sections deal with Christian conduct—how we live as a result of salvation by grace and of Christ's redeeming work. For example, in Ephesians 1 to 3 we find the doctrinal statements and in 4 to 6 the ethical teachings. Ephesians 4 begins, "I urge you to live a life worthy of the calling you have received."

In the letter to the Philippians the teaching about

Christian conduct appears in 1:27: "Whatever happens, conduct yourselves in a manner worthy of the gospel of Christ."

The apostles continually reminded those who troubled the early Christians that faithful obedience and holy living is inseparable from salvation by faith (see, for example, Romans 1:5, 16:26; 1 Peter 1:26 and 13-25, 2:11, 12, etc.).

From the letter to the Romans it is clear that confusion had been born and was growing among the Christians. Paul reacted strongly. But other kinds of trouble mentioned in this letter are also spoken of in the epistle to the Colossians.

The Example of the Colossians

The apostle Paul warns the Colossians (2:4) about "fine-sounding arguments." Luring Christians by beautiful words or interesting theories or by a variety of philosophies reminds one of the ideologies which have spread throughout the world today. This sort of deception and enticement has been a reality since the beginning of the church. It is in this realm that confusion can best gain control of the hearts and minds of Christians. Paul writes in more detail:

> See to it that no one takes you captive through hollow and deceptive philosophy, which depends on human tradition and the basic principles of this world rather than on Christ. For in Christ all the fullness of the Deity lives in bodily form, and you have been given fullness in Christ, who is the head over every power and authority. Colossians 2:8-10.

Therefore do not let anyone judge you by what you

> eat or drink, or with regard to a religious festival, a New Moon celebration or a Sabbath day. These are a shadow of the things that were to come; the reality, however, is found in Christ. Do not let anyone who delights in false humility and the worship of angels disqualify you for the prize. Such a person goes into great detail about what he has seen, and his unspiritual mind puffs him up with idle notions. He has lost connection with the Head.
>
> Colossians 2:16-19a.

Paul warns the Colossians in regard to two things. First, he warns them about philosophy. Doctrine and human wisdom together tend to turn believers from the simplicity they have in Christ (2 Corinthians 11:3), and from the fullness they have in him.

> For in Christ all the fullness of the Deity lives in bodily form, and you have been given fullness in Christ, who is the head over every power and authority.
>
> Colossians 2:9, 10.

The sages and philosophers of the first century confused the Christians in their simple faith in the divine person of Jesus Christ, the perfect Savior. These persons taught that Christians needed to add to this faith a knowledge which would permit them to become part of the highest intellectual and spiritual circles. The number of these "gnostics" was growing rapidly. They were teaching salvation by knowledge rather than by Jesus Christ. To them the Lord of glory was only one philosopher among many others. And some Christians became confused in their faith, seduced by systems of thought and human teachings which led them far from God and from salvation.

Second, ordinary Christian life and conduct were

also deeply affected, at times even completely perverted. Colossians 2:16-23 and 3:1-25 speak of this. Paul presents two choices. *We can hold fast firmly and exclusively to Jesus Christ and his salvation and live in the peace, joy, humility, and reality of the life in Christ* (Colossians 2:17). Or we can put ourselves under the yoke of others—masterminds, philosophers, and ideologists. Now, instead of living an abundant life, we are hemmed in. We are slaves to all sorts of regulations and limitations, to teachings and rituals which must be followed to the letter. What a poor excuse for a Christian life! It's exactly the opposite of a Christian life in its freedom and fullness (Colossians 2:20-23). It is another manifestation of legalism and ritualism. These turn people away from Jesus Christ and confuse the hearts of believers by burdening them with human, pagan ideas which only seem wise.

"So be careful."

A number of young Christians today are led away from their faith by philosophical ideas they learn in high school or college. The Protestant churches today too often give the impression of being "intellectual"—composed mainly of believers who are filled with doubts about the Bible and their faith. Such persons are far from the fullness of life in Jesus Christ. Their daily lives, their personal relationship with God, and their religion is without substance.

The Example of the Corinthians

We will limit ourselves here to Paul's first epistle to the Corinthians, because it is a typical case of those who confuse a church.

The apostle had finished his letter to the Christians of Rome by giving a strict warning against "those who cause divisions." Rarely did he express himself with such vigor.

> I urge you, brothers, to watch out for those who cause divisions and put obstacles in your way that are contrary to the teaching you have learned. Keep away from them. For such people are not serving our Lord Christ, but their own appetites. By smooth talk and flattery they deceive the minds of naive people. Romans 16:17, 18.

Paul was the principal founder of the Corinthian church with the help of Priscilla and Aquila who were already there (see Acts 18:1-18). When Paul wrote the first Corinthian letter, many groups and rival parties had developed within the church. Each group thought itself more right than the other. This was troubling the minds of the believers and dividing the church. Paul wrote,

> What I mean is this: One of you says, "I follow Paul"; another, "I follow Apollos"; another, "I follow Cephas"; still another, "I follow Christ." So Paul makes a strong restatement of the question. "Is Christ divided?" 1 Corinthians 1:12-13a.

From where did this crisis of opposing parties in the Corinthian church come? Theologians have various ideas about it. In his book *L'église au présent* (The Church in the Present), pastor Alphonse Maillot mentions gossip and personal rivalries—the unspiritual ambitions of certain church members which one is led to think of in reading Romans 16:17, 18. In Corinth one finds not only theological disputes, but also scandals in the lives of persons who were still part of the congregation. In addition to jealousy and disputes in this church (1 Corinthians 3:3), one finds immorality worse than among the pagans (1 Corinthians 5).

It's bad news when people in a Christian community argue over who is "right," while others in the congregation accept immorality as consistent with the Christian life. We can understand why Paul writes, "Expel the wicked man from among you" (1 Corinthians 5:13).

But permissiveness was not the only cause of trouble among the Christians. All of 1 Corinthians 7 is given to the question of marriage and celibacy. It seems that there were many different opinions about this in the church, so that they wrote to Paul for counsel and advice concerning it.

The differences of opinion among the believers was so severe that they were also taking each other to court. This was upsetting a number of them. Paul had been informed about these conflicts and responded with his opinion (1 Corinthians 6).

The relationship of believers in Corinth to society's pagan customs provided a logical setting for trouble. Some used these relationships, such as eating food offered to idols, to make difficulties for other members of the congregation (see 1 Corinthians 8-10). Paul counsels them: "Do not cause anyone to stumble, whether Jews, Greeks or the church of God" (1 Corinthians 10:32).

What an abundance of issues to confuse this church at Corinth! But notice Paul's commending words at the beginning of this letter:

I always thank God for you because of his grace given

you in Christ Jesus. For in him you have been enriched in every way—in all your speaking and in all your knowledge—because our testimony about Christ was confirmed in you. Therefore you do not lack any spiritual gift as you eagerly wait for our Lord Jesus Christ to be revealed. 1 Corinthians 1:4-7.

This very congregation so blessed in Christ, seems to have the greatest problem with spiritual gifts and their use. Paul used three chapters to help them find in their worship and meetings an orderliness and conduct worthy of God, and so to again find peace; "For God is not a God of disorder but of peace" (1 Corinthians 14:33).

People often have a false idea of spiritual gifts—what they are, why God gives them and to whom, and of how they should be desired and accepted. Paul closes 1 Corinthians 12—14 with some precise advice. If followed, it would help all Christian groups avoid many internal difficulties and misunderstandings:

Therefore, my brothers, be eager to prophesy, and do not forbid speaking in tongues. But everything should be done in a fitting and orderly way. 1 Corinthians 14:39, 40.

We could also look at the powerful 15th chapter. It speaks about the resurrection and of minds which become troubled through trick questions about the resurrection (1 Corinthians 15:12, 13, 33-35).

Paul's second Corinthian letter gives us also much food for thought about troubles in the church and those who cause them. It seems that in this letter, more than in any other, Paul must defend and justify his ministry. He must also dare to speak of "some who commend themselves" (2 Corinthians 10:12); of those who "want an opportunity" (11:12) and of those who are "false apostles," "deceitful workmen" and servants of Satan (11:13-15). Like the apostle John, Paul uses vigorous language to address those who claim to know God and even to love him, but who are nothing but "liars" (see 1 John 1:4, 9, 18, 19, 26; and 4:20, 21).

"I am writing these things to you about those who are trying to lead you astray" (1 John 2:26).

Other Examples

Paul's letters show that from the first years of the church some have worked confusion in the faith of Christians, disturbed their peace, and destroyed their assurance.

Let's beware, though! Don't misunderstand! We dare not confuse the troubled consciences of church members with feelings of conviction brought by the word of God and the Holy Spirit. The latter is not a harmful "trouble" but a "happy sorrow" which we never regret, for it moves us toward repentance and faith. This is what Paul explains to the Corinthians:

> Godly sorrow brings repentance that leads to salvation and leaves no regret, but worldly sorrow brings death. See what this godly sorrow has produced in you. 2 Corinthians 7:10, 11.

The trouble and confusion I'm addressing is not this inward work of the Holy Spirit. Rather, it is the outward work of liars and deceivers. As Paul reminds his readers in one of his pastoral letters:

The Spirit clearly says that in later times some will

abandon the faith and follow deceiving spirits and things taught by demons. Such teachings come through hypocritical liars, whose consciences have been seared as with a hot iron. 1 Timothy 4:1, 2.

Many theologians think that these "later times" began with the ascension of the Lord Jesus (Hebrews 1:2). If so, we can understand why the church had from its beginning so many false teachers confusing the believers; furthermore, we can expect them to continue to appear until the return of the Lord.

As we page through the New Testament, we see that troubles, and those who brought them into the church, multiplied during the first decades. This is both described and predicted in the letters to the seven churches in Revelation 2 and 3.

The letter to the Hebrews mentions many things which trouble the consciences and hearts of Christians. It is normal for Christians of Jewish origin to ask questions about the fulfillment of promises previously made by God; their concern about the abolition of sacrifices under the new covenant is a valid one. No doubt certain teachers exploited these legitimate concerns as a means of turning the Christians from their faith. This may explain the firm language of this Hebrew letter.

The apostle James underscores the fact that the tongue causes much harm among believers. With the tongue someone can pretend to have faith without producing works to demonstrate it. This is a source of trouble. When the tongue is a "fire, a world of evil," when it praises and also curses, what destruction it brings in the church! (James 2, 3).

James adds, "Do not slander one another," (4:11,

12) and "Don't grumble against each other, brothers, or you will be judged" (5:9).

He gives very definite counsel for achieving harmony and peace in the local congregation and in the church in general. One finds a similar emphasis in the letters of Peter. He writes,

> But there were also false prophets among the people, just as there will be false teachers among you. They will secretly introduce destructive heresies ... and will bring the way of truth into disrepute.
> 2 Peter 2:1, 2.

The verses following this are even stronger and end with a solemn warning. He writes with a vigor which was perhaps formerly difficult to accept. Today, however, when some church leaders live openly immoral lives, its realism is striking.

"They promise them freedom, while they themselves are slaves of depravity" (2 Peter 2:19). One thinks of "churches for homosexuals," not only in America or in the Scandanavian countries, but also in France.

In 2 Peter 3 the apostle announces the arrival of scoffers. They make fun of Christ's return and help to confuse the Christians' belief in the promises of God's Word. Peter invites his readers to be more holy in their life and conduct so they will be found "spotless, blameless and at peace with him" (2 Peter 3:11-14).

Peter recognizes that everything is not easy to understand in the prophecies concerning the end times (eschatology). He writes, in a brotherly way, of Paul's epistles: "His letters contain some things that are hard to understand, which ignorant and unstable people distort, as they do other Scriptures, to their own destruction" (2 Peter 3:16).

No doubt many of the early believers would have liked to have known the exact time and precise order of events which will precede and accompany the return of the Lord Jesus. Even the apostles and disciples of the Lord showed their curiosity by their questions to Jesus. But such questions remain unanswered.

The last two verses of Peter's second epistle are another warning—Christians should be on guard about the return of Christ and not let themselves be led astray. The expression "be carried away" shows the risk run by all those who let themselves be troubled or shaken by teachings which go beyond what the Scripture says. This warning is certainly valid today, even if the church has never before been so near to the return of our beloved Lord and Savior, Jesus Christ!

John's epistles confirm the warnings of the other apostles. He writes about those who lead astray other Christians (1 John 2:26). His concern is about the destruction wrought among believers by "antichrists," liars who deny the Father and the Son. To those who may let themselves be troubled by the messages of such persons, John gives a test to use:

> Dear friends, do not believe every spirit, but test the spirits to see whether they are from God, because many false prophets have gone out into the world. This is how you can recognize the Spirit of God: Every spirit that acknowledges that Jesus Christ has come in the flesh is from God, but every spirit that does not acknowledge Jesus is not from God. This is the spirit of the antichrist. 1 John 4:1-3.

It is clear that he is speaking of the incarnation of the Son of God, of the mystery of his miraculous birth, of the fact that Jesus Christ was truly human and truly God. How many people have stumbled over this "stone"! How many people have listened to the ideas of doubters—like Eve listened to the serpent's voice? And how many believers have lost their faith because of having listened to and followed those who denied Christ's divinity?

How many people have been confused in their faith from that time on by these sowers of doubt and unbelief! But the word of God and of the apostle John gives us the secret of the victory in faith: it is to confess openly before others and before the invisible powers the name of Jesus as the Son of God (1 John 5:1ff.).

In John's second letter he calls for a complete separation from deceivers who trouble people's consciences (vv. 7-9). His third letter treats a different subject: persons in the church who, like Diotrephes, trouble the believers and the congregation by their pride and hunger for power (vv. 9-11).

As for Jude, he seriously warns against those who already then were slipping in among the Christians: "They are godless men, who change the grace of our God into a license for immorality and deny Jesus Christ our only Sovereign and Lord" (v. 4).

There is a battle to wage in the church "for the faith that was once for all entrusted to the saints" (v. 3): a necessary battle, because there always have been and always will be evil persons, such as spoken of in Jude 5 to 19. The secret of the victory of faith is always the same: to stand firm in God and in his love (vv. 20-25; see also 1 John 5:18-21).

The Revelation of John informs and warns us concerning those who from the beginning troubled the church in general as well as specific congregations. It is significant to read about Ephesus: "You have tested those who claim to be apostles but are not, and have found them false" (Revelation 2:2).

To the church at Smyrna he speaks of "those who say they are Jews and are not, but are a synagogue of Satan" (2:9); they slander the believers.

God reproaches the church at Pergamum because it has in its midst "people ... who hold to the teaching of Balaam" (2:14) and others "who hold to the teaching of the Nicolaitans" (2:15). The latter was a more obscure name for those who trouble the church by their teaching and their impure lives.

At Thyatira, they tolerate "that woman Jezebel, who calls herself a prophetess" (2:20). The verses which follow show that he speaks of an influence leading to immorality.

In chapter 3 one finds "those who are of the synagogue of Satan, who claim to be Jews though they are not, but are liars" (3:9). This concerns persons from within the church at Philadelphia who confuse and undermine its life.

Thus, of the seven churches of Asia, only Sardis (3:1-6) does not merit this reproach from the Lord of letting itself be troubled by false witness. But wait! In verse 4 there is a clear reference—not without reason—to those with "soiled clothes."

As for the church at Laodicea (Revelation 3:14-22), nothing is clearly stated about such a harmful influence; but one can assume it to have been at work there as well.

So we finish this rapid survey of the New Testament teachings about those who confuse the church. More than one reader will probably be surprised, as I was, to realize how numerous such persons were and how continually they were at work. So it is not surprising that we find such troublemakers in the church in each century, and especially in our day—in these "last days."

2

DIFFICULTIES IN THE CHURCH TODAY

OUR brief survey of the New Testament showed us that troublemakers appeared wherever the church was established. Now it would be logical to search church history to see if this is repeated—where? when? how? why? and by whom?

I do not feel competent enough in church history to do this. Furthermore, limitations of this booklet require me to be concise, and thus to limit our study. I will leave, then, to a specialist in church history the task of writing a counterpart to the New Testament experience. Nevertheless, a quick survey of 19 centuries of history confirm what happened in the first century. Fanatical and decisive individuals

divisive!

have periodically brought confusion and trouble into local churches and into Christianity as a whole. The circumstances were, of course, often quite different. However, the same types of troubles and the same types of troublemakers are found throughout history and up to the present.

During the last 20 centuries, all sorts of movements have sprung up in the church. These include some disastrous troubles, but also movements of God's Spirit—for example, the great Reformation of the 16th century and the renewals which preceded and followed it.

It is a difficult and delicate task to make value judgments on the persons and movements which have influenced the faith and life of the church.

So we invite you to read the following pages carefully and with goodwill. Our study of the Scriptures in chapter 1 has shown us the facts surrounding the early church. We have noted also the warnings given by the apostles. When we address matters that trouble believers today, we take up a burning issue but do not want to hurt anyone or be misunderstood. What we present in chapter 2 falls more in the area of spiritual counsel than in the area of controversy and argument. May each reader refuse to argue but rather strive to profit personally from these pages. They were written with calmness and love.

We will try to classify problems and troubles in several groups, although these may overlap. It will be impossible to completely separate one case from another of the same type. We will try our best to be clear.

Pardon me for sometimes using "we" and sometimes "I." In both cases the same author is writing. However, I sometimes feel so concerned, or the example given is so much a part of my own personal experience, that I feel obligated to use the personal pronoun "I" to avoid any ambiguity. At other times, I state a known fact, a general rule, a finding that others have made or an opinion I share with many others in our evangelical Mennonite churches. This often reflects the great biblical pacifist Anabaptist movement of the 16th century. In cases such as these the pronoun "we" is used.

The New Testament texts reviewed in chapter 1 provide a plan to follow step by step. But these texts were not written for a systematic study of the problems of the churches. Furthermore, the times and circumstances have changed. Although the burning questions and issues for us are not completely identical to those of the first century, they are closely related.

In the first Christian communities, questions of form, of tradition, of rules, and of law played a large role. The concern to be submissive to the new covenant as well as to the old gave birth to many confrontations in the church and to many troubled consciences. So we begin by examining legalism, as well as ritualism and sacramentalism. Many ethical problems (in morals and in daily life) are connected to these three.

Legalism, Ritualism, and Sacramentalism

The word "legalism" doesn't exist in the Bible. But hundreds of times one finds the word "law" used in a variety of ways. Neither is the word "ritualism" found in the Bible, nor "sacramentalism" or its root, "sacrament."

Their definitions, according to Webster, are:

Legalism—principles and practices characterizing the theological doctrine of strict conformity to a code of deeds and observances.

Ritualism—adherence or observance of a ritual or ritualistic forms; often excessive devotion to prescribed ritual forms in worship.

Sacramentalism—doctrine and use of sacraments, especially the attaching of great importance to sacraments; the doctrine that sacraments are inherently efficacious and indispensable to salvation and capable of conferring grace on a recipient's soul.

Many troublemakers in the church today associate these three things (even if unconsciously) with their conceptions of the Christian life.

We will not study these three ideas as they concern the Roman Catholic Church. They have, of course, been especially important in shaping religious life within that church. And it is the abandonment of rites and customs in the Catholic Church which upsets the traditional believers. For example, many Catholics are troubled by: the abandonment of Latin, changes in the liturgy, the dropping of the clergical attire, and the fact that the majority of those baptized at birth and confirmed at adolescence no longer regularly practice the sacraments.

The Catholicism which had been bound by tradition, at least as much as by the holy Scriptures, has been overturned by theological thought. This is especially true since Vatican II. During this historic meeting, Catholic leaders questioned the rites and traditions, and even the sacraments.

This is almost the opposite of what is happening

in some other churches. One sees in these groups a return to religious communal life, to the practice of daily liturgies which shape the worship, to rules concerning eating, drinking, and respecting certain days, to required rest on the Sabbath (Saturday). One sees people unquestioningly submit to certain Christian rites in the only form considered valid by a certain denomination. This profoundly troubles many sincere Christians who wish to live lives pleasing to God.

Please do not consider these words as an attack against certain denominations nor as a value judgment on them. Only the Lord can judge. We are disturbed and uneasy when we see how the importance given to form and rules causes confusion in many hearts.

Legalism

Certain aspects of legalism have troubled and still do trouble Christians. We have, among the Anabaptist-Mennonites, a perfectly respectable group called "Amish." Each Amish person must dress in a certain way and follow certain rules which one does not find in the New Testament. This makes us think of Paul's warning to the Colossians concerning those who say: "Do not handle! Do not taste! Do not touch!" (Colossians 2:20-23).

For example, the Anabaptists of Montbeliard, France, were still part of this Amish tradition at the beginning of this century. They prohibited the use of buttons (they were too "worldly") and used only hooks and eyes to fasten their dark-colored clothing. Today one finds, of course, extremes of fashion which it is well to avoid—even common sense would demand it. But why make the wearing of or refusing to wear a certain piece of clothing a doctrine? Modesty is the rule to follow. This does not exclude a little elegance and/or imagination.

Holiness is not tied to length of hair. Neither does clothing for men and women mean what it did in the Orient centuries ago. Let men be men and women be women in the society in which we live, whether in Europe, Africa, or elsewhere. Let them seek to glorify the Lord by their appearance, their attitude, their behavior, as well as by their language—these all are the outer expression of their inner life.

But it is a pity (as well as damaging for the life of the church) that well-intentioned preachers insist that appearance must not change. They fail to realize that such changes may be simply an expression of a change in lifestyle or an adaptation to a different civilization. Why create a fuss when some people doing mission in other cultures need to make changes because of their situation—changes in dress, mode of travel, and family obligations? They are adapting, as Paul said he did in 1 Corinthians 9:19-23.

Legalism is often noticeable by strict rules about how something should be done for all times and civilizations. But in Christ we enjoy freedom from such human-made regulations.

Forms of worship provide another area for legalism to raise its ugly head. We are to worship God in spirit and in truth (John 4:23, 24).

In our understanding of the Scriptures, there is no one right way to worship God in spirit and in truth. According to the New Testament, Christ gave us no one precise way to celebrate the Lord's ordinances—baptism and holy communion. Thus, true worship is lost when restricted to one form.

The Old Testament did prescribe exactly how the tabernacle was to be built, and how the various sorts of sacrifices were to be offered. But the New Testament affirms that all these things were only a shadow of the good things to come: "the reality is in Christ" (Hebrews and Colossians).

One is hurt, then, to see sincere Christians, young and old, being confused by persons who ask them if they were baptized the "right" way. One is saddened to hear someone preaching that there is only one "right" way to be baptized and only one "true sign" of the Holy Spirit's baptism. The Lord Jesus gave us only one standard to judge by: that of mutual love and of spirit fruit.

"Likewise every good tree bears good fruit, but a bad tree bears bad fruit" (Matthew 7:17).

> A new commandment I give you: Love one another. As I have loved you, so you must love one another. All men will know that you are my disciples if you love one another. John 13:34, 35.

Some Christians have completely given up both baptism and communion to keep only the essential part of the gospel message. Two of these groups are the Society of Friends (or Quakers), and the Salvation Army.

The Friends worship mostly in silence and meditation, in spirit and in truth. They emphasize love of neighbor, refusal of violence, and the spirit of peace. The Quakers, along with the Mennonites, were from their beginnings one of the first Christian groups to advocate a peaceful solution to conflict, as did the Christian church in its beginning.

The Salvation Army, unlike the Quakers, has joyful worship services, with much singing and many "hallelujahs." They are known everywhere for their works of charity, social concern, and public evangelism accompanied by singing and instruments. Their motto ("Saved to Serve"), their three-S slogan ("Soup, Soap, Salvation"), their method of evangelism, and their flag depicting the blood of Christ and the fire of the Spirit—all four are marks of these ardent and convinced Christians who have no place for sacraments.

These are two extreme examples in the rainbow of Christian denominations. We know some from the Salvation Army who have gone elsewhere to respond to Jesus' commands to baptize disciples. Sometimes some, because of an inner need, participate in a communion service with another friendly Christian congregation. I do not know of any Quakers who have looked beyond their own group for this sort of answer to a personal aspiration.

So we note the relative unimportance these groups give to certain rules for worship. For them, too, the spirit is more important than the letter (2 Corinthians 3:6).

In some respects Mennonites are very close to the Friends and to the Salvation Army. But they differ from them in this: Mennonites interpret the Bible more literally concerning baptism and communion, but without believing in only one form. Obviously, it's the idea of sacrament itself which is at stake and the role, the place, and the importance of symbols in the church. For example, our Baptist friends do not consider immersion merely a form of baptism having more symbolism and therefore being more desirable than any other form. Rather, they believe immersion *is* the baptism. Without immersion in water, in their view, there is no baptism.

In no way do I oppose immersion. Many times I have myself baptized persons by immersion or have participated in such a service. For example, I participated in a baptismal service in the Chari River in Chad. Here several hundred persons were immersed and emerged to confess their faith before thousands of people. It was so natural for that climate and setting to use immersion for baptism!

In contrast, immersion has sometimes seemed to me artificial and complicated, far from the New Testament pattern both in letter and in spirit! In this I see appear—whether or not one wishes it—a certain form of sacramentalism. Things *must* be done in a certain way to be valid, and the symbol is given priority over the inner spiritual reality. The reality is, of course, in Christ—and not in the symbol.

In no way are we accusing our Baptist friends in general of being troublemakers in our evangelical or Mennonite communities. Mutual bonds of respect and affection link us together. We readily accept the fact of their firm conviction and agree to their practice of immersion according to the leading of their consciences. In the same way, we have our own convictions on other points and try to live accordingly (nonresistance, for example) without trying to impose these on others.

But there are those who trouble certain members of our churches. They seize every opportunity to accuse us of being disobedient to God and his Word because we have not been baptized by immersion. Their attitudes and actions grieve us and make true fellowship difficult. It becomes even more difficult because one learns from others (not from them) that they are trying to exert spiritual pressure.

Their attitude is not Christian nor are they sound teachers. Rather, they uselessly spread trouble in consciences and hearts instead of contributing to peace and to building up the body of Christ.

Baptism and Its Meaning

We have said that to consider immersion as baptism rather than a form of it is, in a way, sacramentalism. It is true that "baptism" comes from the Greek word *baptizein* which means to immerse or to plunge into. However, let us look at some translations and commentaries which are of interest. The Revised Standard Version of Mark 7:3, 4 reads,

> For the Pharisees, and all the Jews, do not eat unless they wash their hands, observing the tradition of the elders; and when they come from the market place, they do not eat unless they purify.[w] themselves; and there are many other traditions which they observe, the washing of cups and pots and vessels of bronze.

The footnote "w" states, "other ancient authorities read *baptize*." The French translation of the Bible, *Bible à la Colombe*, has this same note; in addition, where it says "washing of cups," the word for washing is the same word as baptism.

When we compare various translations, we see important shades of meanings: "ceremonial washing," "washing," "washing [the hands] frequently and thoroughly," "washing their arms as far as the elbow," "sprinkling themselves," "wash . . . in the proper way." (See *New International Version, New English Bible, The Jerusalem Bible,* and *Today's English Version.*)

All of these expressions do not have a direct relation to the baptism of repentance as practiced by John the Baptist nor with baptism as commanded by Jesus Christ. These washings of the body show how the Jews, in order to approach God according to the laws of Moses, needed to purify themselves ritually.

Anyone who has traveled in Africa or in the East has seen how one can wash oneself by pouring a small amount of water carefully on the hands and forearms. The ritual cleansing of the face and body is widespread. The method of baptism is often determined by the amount of water available. Certainly the form is not important, if the goal is attained: for example, symbolizing inner cleansing by Christ, death to the old life of sin and entrance into the new life in Christ.

The baptism of repentance, preached and practiced by John the Baptist and his followers, then by Jesus and his, was a solemn occasion. John baptized where "there was plenty of water" (3:22, 23). This illustrated forcefully the need of being cleansed spiritually and the great amount of purification needed. It was a humbling experience for the one being baptized to go down into water publicly, to let oneself be immersed and to be at the mercy of the one baptizing you (to have a "life-size" ritual cleansing).

But the New Testament does not tell us how baptism was practiced. And no one can say how or where the first 3,000 converts on Pentecost were baptized. At least twice the holy Scriptures, our supreme authority, speak of washing and purification in direct connection with baptism. In Hebrews 10:22 we read,

> Let us draw near to God with a sincere heart in full assurance of faith, having our hearts sprinkled to cleanse us from a guilty conscience and having our bodies washed with pure water.

This does not mean one washes the body of a person during a baptism by immersion. Rather, it is a reference to the ritual washings practiced under the law of Moses by the priests and Levites. Note also the idea of sprinkling.

In 1 Peter 3:21, the writer states clearly that "this water symbolizes baptism that now saves you also— not the removal of dirt from the body but the pledge of a good conscience toward God." Baptism is a symbolizing of a new (right) standing with God.

The apostle Paul interpreted the symbol of baptism as being "buried" with Christ (Romans 6:3, 4 and Colossians 2:12). This is a curious burial because it is done in water, contrary to normal custom (except burial at sea). Paul seems to say that baptism symbolizes death to one's former, sinful life.

It is not in immersion then that one looks for the meaning and reason of Paul's explanation of baptism. And no one should be troubled because of the manner in which they were baptized. The important questions are: Were you baptized at your own request, on the personal confession of your faith in Jesus Christ, with a commitment to live in communion with God and the church through the Holy Spirit?

Note how often the question of baptism brings controversy concerning its form. While there are a thousand ways of practicing the Lord's Supper, no one seems to think it has to be done in exactly the same way the Lord did it. He did it according to the customs of his time—during the meal which commemorates the deliverance from Egypt.

As a symbol, baptism stands for much more than immersion in water. It is the voluntary acceptance of dying with Christ to live with him by the power of the Holy Spirit. As Paul teaches,

> [You are] ... buried with him in baptism and raised with him through your faith in the power of God, who raised him from the dead. Colossians 2:12.
>
> We were therefore buried with him through baptism into death in order that, just as Christ was raised from the dead through the glory of the Father, we too may live a new life. Romans 6:4.

Another relevant passage is Galatians 3:26, 27: "You are all sons of God through faith in Christ Jesus, for all of you who were baptized into Christ have been clothed with Christ."

In these passages Paul does not contradict the teaching about baptism as explained in Hebrews or 1 Peter. The images used are different, but the reality is the same: it is not the act of baptism which produced an effect, even when performed with the most perfect possible symbolism.

The reality is in Christ, and true baptism is immersion in Christ (and not in water). It is spiritual communion with him. We submerge ourselves into his death on the cross for the forgiveness of sin—and emerge from the depths, one with him in his resurrection and victory over death, by the glorious power of God. "We were . . . buried with him [so] . . . we too may live a new life" (Romans 6:4).

Because true baptism is immersion in Christ, the amount of water used to symbolize it is unimportant. Mennonites and other Christians practice it either by sprinkling, pouring, or immersion. The method often reflects the custom, circumstance, or personal conviction of the baptismal candidates. For example, some choose pouring as a reminder of the pouring out of the Holy Spirit on the first Christians (Acts 2:33). The essential is always the inner reality of union with Christ, shown in a holy life.

Baptism of the Holy Spirit, and Spiritual Gifts

Some churches believe that immersion in water is the only way to receive persons into the local congregation. Other churches emphasize the necessity of the baptism of the Holy Spirit and the importance of spiritual gifts. They may believe that the normal evidence of the baptism of the Holy Spirit is speaking in tongues.

We respect persons who are very attached to what they call divine healing. They are convinced that a faithful believer must be physically and mentally healthy. If there is a problem in these areas, they believe it's because of sin. To recover health, the sin must be confessed and forsaken, and then through faith one will be delivered.

Some teach and practice the need to search out carefully in their lives any trace of the occult, any contact with demonic powers, and any sin inherited from ancestors. Then, by confession, personal prayer, laying on of hands, and exorcism, they become Christians who are truly free spiritually.

We could cite many more examples. Some believe and teach that one must observe the Sabbath (Saturday, the seventh day of the week) as the day set apart for the Lord, for rest, worship, and the joy of salvation. They believe that to abandon the seventh day, the Sabbath rest, for the first day of the week (Sunday) is being unfaithful to God's Word and divine order.

We can respect these persons because they have a real concern to practice God's Word and to appropriate its promises. We have friends among them, even if we do not agree with all their concepts and teachings. They tend to give too much weight to certain ideas and texts to the neglect of the teachings of the Bible as a whole.

However, we disagree completely with those who believe that their way is the *only* Christian way to believe and live. This is especially so when they do things by deceitful means. An example is speaking to faithful members of evangelical churches (ours or another) to entice members to join their group. Are there not all around us thousands of people, modern pagans, to win for Christ, rather than to upset by questionable teaching those who are already active members of a church?

These actions are a source of trouble in the midst of evangelical congregations. Their tactless actions and methods are similar to those of dangerous cults. One can, therefore, understand the reactions of large "mainline" churches who come under their deceptive attack.

There is, then, a clear distinction between these two groups: the normal Christian witness of evangelical churches who try their best to announce the gospel of Jesus Christ to people today, and the religious propagandists who seek to uproot Christians from their churches, drawing them away into their own group for their own profit.

Now we want to briefly examine the doctrines and methods of those who make this kind of trouble—who sometimes collaborate with other churches to insert themselves and steal "sheep." Here are some methods we challenge:

a. The Baptism of the Holy Spirit

It is easy to try to systematize and be dogmatic regarding the baptism of the Holy Spirit. This we want to avoid in order to adhere, firmly and wisely, to the entire revelation of God. What does the Scripture say?

Numerous writings are available on the baptism of the Holy Spirit (e.g., *The Spirit of God* by G. Campbell Morgan, and *Catholic Pentecostals* by K. & D. Ranagan). This fact alone indicates that there are many different opinions about it. There are two main opposing ideas.

First, the baptism of the Holy Spirit is a fundamental part of the experience of each person who is converted to Jesus Christ and born anew. This is what John the Baptist is speaking of when he announces:

"I baptize you with water, but he will baptize you with the Holy Spirit" (Mark 1:8 or John 1:33). And Jesus spoke clearly about this baptism when He said: "You must be born again ... unless a man is born of water and the Spirit, he cannot enter the kingdom of God" (John 3:7, 5).

Second, the baptism of the Holy Spirit is sometimes an experience independent from conversion. It includes an empowering for the service of God, a manifestation of spiritual gifts, the most important being the gift of tongues.

Those who hold to this interpretation base their belief on Acts 2 (the story of Pentecost with reference to Joel 2); Acts 8:14 (the Samaritans); Acts 10:44ff. (the pagans); and Acts 19 (the Ephesians). According to these passages the pouring out of the Holy Spirit on the believers is accompanied by speaking in tongues.

We do not want to divide Christians into those "more faithful" or "less faithful" to the word of God. This is not where the problem is. Fortunately, there are faithful believers on both sides. Although they may think differently, they respect each other and love each other in the Lord. So what is the source of the problem?

The problem arises when one of the groups wishes to impose on the other its way of looking at and understanding the Bible. Trouble comes when a certain evangelist, teacher, or speaker builds up a following based on controversy and systematic criticism of other Christians and their churches. The stage is set for confusion when one group pretends to have a monopoly on the truth and looks down on other believers. Let's be willing to admit that others, through their faith and piety, can enrich all the body of Christ.

May we seek to preach Christ crucified, dead for our sins according to the Scriptures, raised for our justification, present with us each day till the end by his Holy Spirit who lives in us, seated at the right hand of God from where he will come to give salvation to those who await him and to judge the living and the dead (Hebrews 9:28, 29 and Romans 4:25).

We believe that he wants for his own an abundant life in communion with him. He calls each child of God (born again by the action of the word of God and of the Holy Spirit) to produce fruit, the fruit of the Spirit. Each one is to do the works which God calls him to so that he may accomplish them to God's glory and live in a manner worthy of him who called him to his kingdom (John 10:10; Galatians 5:22).

This has nothing to do with a judgmental attitude toward others, with the spirit of controversy or competition. Such true believers walk humbly with their God in the joy of salvation, in peace, in justice, in truth (Romans 14:17). Such believers are not the censors or critics of other Christians and of other churches. Rather, they watch over themselves, their own conduct, and personal obedience. They know that they will need to give a personal account to God. If unfaithful, they will be rejected, even after they have preached to others and have done miracles in Christ's name (1 Corinthians 9:27 and 10:12; Matthew 7:21-23).

Thus, they don't let themselves be troubled by those who pretend to know more than they do. But, like the Christians of Berea, they return each day to the word of God, to see whether what they have heard agrees with it. They try to examine all things and to keep what is good (Acts 17:11; 1 Thessalonians 5:21).

b. Concerning Spectacular Gifts

Now we address the trouble caused by teachings and practices concerning spiritual gifts which do not conform to the word of God.

Some have reproached us, in our own congregation, because among our spiritual leaders we do not have the gifts of tongues, healing, and prophecy. This may be true, in their thinking. However, their idea of prophecy and healing is rather far from the biblical meaning of them.

First of all, why set up as "special" certain more spectacular gifts? The list of gifts is not limited to them, and the New Testament does not set up a hierarchy of gifts. One could almost say that the opposite is true! (1 Corinthians 12:4-11 and 27-31). The priority always seems to go to those who contribute to the building up of the church by the teaching of the Word, by wisdom, knowledge, and discernment.

The three principal lists of gifts in Romans 12 and 1 Corinthians 12, are very instructive. They come in this order:

a. According to Romans 12:6-8
 1. Prophesying (word from God)
 2. Serving (spirit of service)
 3. Teaching (of Christian truth)
 4. Encouraging
 5. Contributing (generosity)
 6. Leadership (directing meetings)
 7. Showing mercy (have a heart open to others)

b. According to 1 Corinthians 12:7-10
 1. Message of wisdom
 2. Message of knowledge
 3. Faith
 4. Gift of healing

     5. Miraculous powers
     6. Prophecy
     7. Ability to distinguish between spirits
     8. Ability to speak in different kinds of tongues
     9. Interpretation of tongues

  c. According to 1 Corinthians 12:28
     1. Apostles
     2. Prophets
     3. Teachers
     4. Workers of miracles
     5. Those having gifts of healing
     6. Those able to help others
     7. Those with gifts of administration
     8. Those speaking different kinds of tongues

In the two lists from 1 Corinthians 12, the three spiritual gifts listed in first place are not spectacular. It is only when we come to fourth or fifth place that we find the gifts of healing and performing miracles. And we know how suspect these gifts can be, according to the Lord Jesus himself and also according to certain stories in the book of Acts (see Matthew 7:22, 23; Acts 8:9-11; Acts 19:13-16; and 1 Corinthians 13:12).

Let us look at 1 Corinthians 12:29, 30. Note that these probing questions call for the negative response: "Are all apostles? Are all prophets? Are all teachers? Do all work miracles? Do all have gifts of healing? Do all speak in tongues? Do all interpret?" Let us dare then to answer honestly, as a logical and sane interpretation of the Scripture leads us to do: "Certainly not!"

And let us recognize that this very clear verse *invalidates* the teaching which says that speaking in tongues is *the* sign of the baptism of the Holy Spirit.

We have known too many believers, young and

old, who have been tormented because someone has upset them with this problem, telling them that every Christian baptized by the Holy Spirit must speak in tongues. This is not true. And many pentecostals and charismatics, holding to what the Bible teaches, agree with us on this. But not all have this same loyalty to the Scriptures and to other believers.

In my youth I was a fervent, active Christian. So I deeply desired to live all that the Lord offered, and sought to speak in tongues. A certain eminently respected servant of God, still living, can testify to this. I never received this gift, and I had to accept by faith that this was okay. I submitted to God, to the one who is Lord, and to the Spirit, who performs all things and who distributes gifts to each one, as he wishes, for the common good (see 1 Corinthians 12:4-7, 11).

Let no one then be troubled if he or she has sought long and sincerely to receive from the Holy Spirit a certain gift for the common good and has not received it. The Lord alone is judge of what is for the "common good." He knows best the manner in which he wishes to give gifts and to use each of his children in the church.

I have often heard persons speaking in tongues or singing in tongues, and have sometimes been greatly blessed. Other times I have been blessed little or not at all. I am not the only one with such experiences. Speaking in tongues is not the most important thing. Love is the most important in communing with the God who is love (see 1 Corinthians 13 and 1 John 4:7, 8.) And God can at any time give to his children, whoever they may be, gifts that he has until now refused. What joy and fullness to live in such abundance and such submission to his will!

c. A Troublesome Misunderstanding

Some take pleasure in feeding the misunderstanding that God wants all believers to have the same experience of Christian faith. God never leads his people to be uniformly alike, as some would claim. He does not give all the same experiences nor the same spiritual gifts. He teaches nowhere in his Word that all true Christians, men or women, young or old, must speak in tongues.

The 120 persons in the upper room were all "filled with the Holy Spirit and began to speak in other tongues as the Spirit enabled them" (Acts 2:4). However, after the conversion of the 3,000 persons who were added to the church this same day of Pentecost (v. 41), there is no mention of speaking in tongues. Note that their spiritual experience and their Christian life are characterized in Acts 2:42-47 by their devotion to the apostles' teaching, to fellowship, to the breaking of bread, and to prayer.

Neither is there any mention of tongues in Acts 4:4 and 23-31. The end of chapter 4 describes this new society in Jerusalem—the first Christian church.

The emphasis throughout Acts is on a life of Christian discipleship in a local group where Christians loved and cared for each other. That is the best standard for measuring spirituality. This general rule is not contradicted by a few special cases of new believers who, in special circumstances, spoke in tongues when they received the Holy Spirit (Acts 10:44-48 and 19:1-7). In Acts 8 it is not specifically stated that the Samaritans spoke in tongues, but we may suppose they did. If they did, this may have been a sign that in Christ they who once were outside God's faith community (Israel) could now belong to it.

Believers who are troubled about obtaining this gift at any price must give themselves to the Lord and what he wants for them personally. The other side of this misunderstanding is that someone may be content with a mediocre Christian life; they may live without joy or gladness, as if such a life were enough.

But to believe is not enough. There must be growth. We dare not be content to believe in Jesus for the forgiveness of sin and the assurance of salvation and stop with this. Each day we must seek to live in communion with him by the Holy Spirit, to "grow in the grace and knowledge of our Lord and Savior Jesus Christ" (2 Peter 3:18). Each child of God is called to this—there are no exceptions. Then all will know fullness of life and receive the spiritual gift—or gifts—which are destined for them.

It is confusing to equate the receiving of a spiritual gift and the abundance of life offered by God with salvation in Jesus Christ. We must continually aspire to this fullness of life in Christ. We dare not neglect the spiritual gifting which our heavenly Father wants for each of his children according to their diversity and his riches. The Corinthians were invited by Paul to desire above all the gift of prophecy. This is the ability to transmit with power the word of God, making it real as the prophets did. It is speaking for God, before God, and from him to his people. Paul probably told them this because they were seeking too much the other spiritual gifts, rather than obedience to the clearly understood word of God.

The most "spiritual" of Paul's letters, Ephesians, does not even mention spiritual gifts. But it is entirely consecrated to the deepening of life "in Christ." In chapter 2 he says, "You were dead . . . but now in Jesus Christ . . . you too are being built together to become a dwelling in which God lives by his Spirit." The goal is a full and victorious life described especially in Ephesians 3:14-21.

All spiritual gifts given to the church are intended to lead each believer in continual growth toward the "measure of the fullness of Christ" (Ephesians 4:1-16). And in the rules of conduct given next, we find this pearl which encloses the secret of the victorious Christian life: "Be filled with the Spirit," independently of any particular gifts given to one or to another, for the common good. The example of the church at Ephesus ought to be the envy of every disciple of Jesus Christ.

Sickness and Divine Healing

". . . and I left Trophimus sick in Miletus" (2 Timothy 4:20).

This word of the apostle Paul is most disappointing and mysterious because no explanation follows it. Paul, perhaps more than any other, had healed the sick by prayer and the laying on of hands. He had even brought back to life one dead person (Eutychus in Acts 20:7-12). But he has left us no theory about faith healing. James, in his epistle (5:13-16), told Christians what to do when someone is sick; but Paul wrote nothing similar. Neither did

John. And Peter encouraged Christians to bear their suffering and to commit their souls to the Creator in doing good. The promise of 1 Peter 5:10, 11, is characteristic: we are called to eternal glory, after we have suffered for a while! The kind of suffering is not specified, but we believe it includes physical suffering and sickness. This is something which deeply troubles many Christians.

Such trouble is greatly increased when sick persons are told that their illness results from sin in their life (which is often not true). Their anguish is further increased when, after having tried to "make things right" with God and others, the sickness remains and healing does not come.

Then "those people who throw you into confusion" appear and deepen the suffering and despair by accusing the sick one of lacking faith (quoting Bible verses). They may even accuse the sick one of some sin of his ancestors or of some connection to the occult from which the person must be delivered.

This is serious, because there may be some truth in these statements. But the truth is mixed with unscriptural, harmful generalizations. One can always take one or two verses out of context to support such an argument. But it will not stand up under a careful examination of the Scripture as a whole. And it is the whole biblical message to which we must adhere.

a. Some Facts

I personally knew a woman whose life from birth was affected by a serious congenital heart ailment. She lived at a slow pace without ever complaining or accusing God. Rather the opposite. She loved the

Lord and his Word. She made the best possible use of the little strength she had. She prayed much. She loved to have us visit her, and she would participate with us in discussing a Bible passage, in singing, and in prayer. But she dreaded the visits of certain of God's servants. Under the pretext of spiritual counseling, they would question her, trying to discover the causes of her illness in order to exorcise them.

Paul may have been an expert in understanding the human mind, the occult, or the consequences of the sins of ancestors. But even so, he left Trophimus sick at Miletus (without accusing him of hidden sin or of a sinful heritage). Job, a righteous man of whom God boasted before Satan, was accused of having "something not right in his life"! What cruel ignorance, what irony, what total misunderstanding of the ways of God, ways often hidden and mysterious! For example, the man reported in John 9:1-12 was born blind "so that the work of God might be displayed in his life."

I know that someone could object (some have already done so!) by saying, "But Job and the man born blind were miraculously healed in the end, for the glory of God!" Certainly, and thanks be to God for having preserved their example in his Word to enlighten our minds, console our hearts, and encourage our faith!

But God teaches us other things in his Word. And they seem to contradict the above. However, they are complementary rather than contradictory. They help us to be wiser and more careful when we face sickness and other trials. Trophimus, left sick at Miletus by Paul, is an illustration. Many other Scripture passages invite us to be humble before the sovereign God, the God who does and permits to be done what he wills without needing to be accountable to anyone. Is he not more honored by the humble submission and total confidence of his children, than by their demands based on promises as they "besiege the throne of grace?" (a nonbiblical expression which must be offensive to our God who is love and wisdom). He has no need of being "besieged" to answer prayer for his distressed children and give them his best. Such a "siege" is rather the sign of a person who wishes to impose his own will instead of finding God's good, pleasing, and perfect will (Romans 12:1, 2). Nevertheless, we should not forget the persistant prayer of faith (Luke 18:1-8).

Too many well-intentioned Christians ignore or scorn the ending of Hebrews 11. All the persons mentioned there are "heroes of the faith," even those who "were tortured and refused to be released, so that they might gain a better resurrection" (v. 35). Verse 39 is clear: "These were all commended for their faith, yet none of them received what had been promised."

This is not only what the holy Scripture affirms, it also is a fact. This truth is often seen today in the lives of believers. They are as firm in their faith as they are tested by illness in their bodies. They live in humble submission and in unshakable confidence. I could cite many examples, past and present, of brothers and sisters, whose faith in suffering strengthened the faith of those around them. Rather than pressing God for a "cure at any price," they accept the lot that God has for them here on earth, while waiting in hope for this "something better" which God has planned and spoken of in Hebrews 11:40.

b. A Testimony

Permit me to give a personal testimony. About 20 years ago my wife was dying of cancer. There had been a joyful period of remission when we believed she was cured. Then came a relapse, and the doctor felt sure that the outcome would be fatal. Instead of running here and there to specialists recommended to us by loving and well-meaning friends, we redoubled our prayers. Probably thousands of brothers and sisters in Christ were interceding with the Savior for us, asking him to intervene with power for his glory. But the illness progressed relentlessly, and my wife became slowly weaker. She was suffering much pain, but was fully aware and confident that God would direct in all things.

A Javanese brother, well-known for his participation in the Indonesian revival and for his gift of healing, informed us that he was praying to God for us in a special way. We knew each other well, and he knew of our responsibilities in the Lord's service. He said that he wanted to visit us on his way to the Mennonite World Conference, since he would be going through Europe. He asked if we would agree to have him lay hands on the sick one, in the name of the Lord, and was confident that the Lord willed her healing.

We saw this first of all as an extraordinary sign of the affection surrounding us through a chain of prayers around the world (friends in America and Africa were praying for us too). We also saw this as a sign that the Lord was going to do something extraordinary! And we quickly answered, "Yes."

Brother Hadi arrived. He went upstairs to my wife's room and talked with her about the word of God, about its promises. He asked Helen if she believed, searching in a brotherly way to understand her spiritual situation. He was preparing to experience with her the marvelous answer to prayer which an instant miraculous healing is (as in the Gospels or in Acts). Then, after a fervent prayer and his laying hands on her, he called upon the Lord with praise and thanksgiving, asking for Helen's healing.

After a moment, he stopped. Nothing happened. He went downstairs, then went up again to her room. Silently he looked at her thin but peaceful face. He sat near her bed, took her hand, and with strong emotion, said, "Sister Helen, I no longer have the assurance that God wishes to heal you. I came to bring you something from God. But it's you who have brought good to me. I feel that you are so submitted to the Lord's will, so confident in his love, so committed to him, that I can want nothing better for you. May peace continue to be with you and to fill your heart! Good-bye! Stay near him!"

Hadi got up, sad and happy at the same time. What a disappointment for those who, knowing about his visit, were expecting her healing! Several weeks later she went to be with "the Shepherd and Overseer of [our] souls" (1 Peter 2:25). My children and I, and my dear sister Anna—who had been so much help to us—were kneeling around Helen when she left to join the one who had so loved her and who was ready to welcome her. By his side "there will be no more death or mourning or crying or pain, for the old order of things has passed away" (Revelation 21:4). Her sufferings had ended, and this was the answer to prayer that God gave us, not according to our wishes or will, but according to his. And he is wise. We wept much after that. I cried and grieved before the Lord, but I never doubted his perfect love and faithfulness.

That I am still living 20 years later, I know I owe to his grace alone. Several times he has shown me his goodness—when he made me healthy again after surgery; when he spared me from having to submit to a difficult treatment which the doctors had thought necessary; when he gave me enough strength to serve him even when my heart was thought unable to function anymore. In the last 30 years the elders of my congregation have come several times to lay hands on me in his name. I have learned to completely give myself up to him so that he may decide. It is marvelous!

But I also need to learn that the Lord is sovereign (see Ezekiel 24:15ff.). He can heal when and how he wants. But he doesn't always heal—he can have other plans for us.

c. Do Not Let Your Hearts Be Troubled!

These words of the Lord Jesus to his disciples before leaving them can serve as our title for the last part of this section. We see them reported in John 14:1 and 27.

I dedicate them to all those who are troubled by the problems of sickness, suffering, death, and the life beyond: "Do not let your hearts be troubled. Trust in God; trust also in me."

To all those who trust in him, the Lord says something like this in his word: trust me, now and always, no matter what happens. Don't doubt my love when I don't answer your prayers like you hoped and believed I would. Never forget that I can always heal your woes here on earth. But don't lose sight of the fact that I don't always do it. I have my reasons, and one day you'll understand. Trust me. And then....

"Always giving thanks to God the Father for everything, in the name of our Lord Jesus Christ" (Ephesians 5:20).

To be obedient to this word, I had to go to my wife's grave and give thanks. So I know what I'm talking about when I advise others to do the same.

In our local church and elsewhere we have often experienced faith healing, but never in the same manner. One time it happened by the laying on of hands and anointing with oil during a regular church service. A brother requested healing in response to a sermon given that day without the preacher knowing what the sick brother had been experiencing. Once a sister with a totally different kind of illness was healed in a prayer group. Another time it was in a hospital, with a mother at the bedside of her child who had been in a coma for several weeks. Three friends had come with me for prayer and the laying on of hands. The non-Christian father and the doctors had agreed to this, for they could do nothing more. The Lord answered marvelously. To him be the glory!

But it is not always thus. All sick Christians do not ask for the help of the Christian community in this way. Other families seek outside the local church for help. And why? The Lord answers or does not answer, and it does not depend on how he has been asked.

In any case we must learn to be more dependent on him in complete confidence and faithful obedience. We dare not let ourselves be troubled, not by events nor by persons, even though they be "men of God."

Fanatics and Imposters

Fortunately, the word of God records the severe expressions the inspired writers used to warn the first-generation Christians against fanatics and imposters. They came among them to abuse their good faith, feeding on them while meeting with them, arguing about words, provoking disunity.... "Stay away from such people!" Paul wrote. Peter, John, and Jude are not gentle with these false teachers, these hypocrites, these liars (see 2 Peter 2:1-3; 1 John 2:4, 22, 23 and 4:20, 21; Jude vv. 4, 6-19). Those three words—false teachers, hypocrites and liars—seem incompatible with Christianity and life in the Christian community. But it is this community which is spoken of here, and these persons claim to belong to it. Some even teach there, relying on personal revelation—"God told me" ... "The Lord spoke to me" ... "The Holy Spirit revealed to me that...."

Such words are impressive. A weak Christian or a new believer who is searching for a "real experience" of God's power in answer to prayer cannot help reacting favorably. Here is someone with something for me, they think. Here is someone who truly knows the Lord! Our preachers and elders never talk like this, they think.

And so they listen to an "inspired" message; they give attention to the ideas presented, if not swallowing them whole! They follow this "powerful evangelist" who knows how to skillfully undermine the leaders of Christian communities and churches.

And finally, people give generously and liberally to promote the cause of this "true gospel," so well presented. They give so that this "word" can grow and develop for the salvation and healing of many! They write letters with checks enclosed to join the crowd of those who offer "special" prayers for the healing of such and such a person.

a. Methods Unworthy of the Gospel

We don't need to go into detail about this, since others have already done so. Here we only wish to point out that methods unworthy of the gospel are being used to attempt to transmit the gospel. The end does not justify the means. One cannot copy the commercial marketing specialists and prey upon the weakness of people to attract "clients," to create a "market," and to obtain large sums of money.

We know good Christians who don't realize that they are being manipulated for "a good cause" (to preach the gospel, to heal the sick, to save souls). Unknowingly, they are manipulated by letters and brochures, radio and television, and even the Word. They are no longer free to decide, with thanksgiving to God, how much to give to God's work through their congregation or denomination. No, they are told by an outsider what they must do and give. Further, they are guaranteed that for a certain sum of money there will not only be results here on earth, but also in heaven. This exploits people's readiness to believe. And good-hearted, gullible Christians let themselves be ensnared.

These well-known "preachers" have such an impact that some Christians don't even think about asking for advice from their own pastors or elders. Have any of our leaders ever had someone ask: "Brother _____, I heard this; or I read this; or I received this.... It impressed me. But what do you think? Could we talk about it at church? Could we look at this together by studying the Bible and praying?"

No, these "sellers of the gospel," these "gospel imposters" never encourage their listeners to ask advice of the leaders in their local churches. By their self-confident manner they impose their authority on people for whom they are not responsible before God. They impose themselves on Christians who are already responsible members of a flock, joined with brothers and sisters in a church where the word of God is regularly preached.

This is blackmail, enticement, and abuse of confidence.

Who can say what trouble this can cause in evangelical communities, or what poisonous fruits it can produce internally or externally—double-dealing, pretence, suspicion, division. Such "ensnared" persons continue to be members of their local churches. However, it is from elsewhere that they receive their assignments, their orders, the teachings they consider valid.

b. *Distinctions to Make*

There are distinctions to make. And it's important to make them.

We wrote at the beginning of this book that we would not be discussing the cults or sects. We hope that all our readers understand such cults enough that they are not troubled by them (e.g., "Christ of Montfavet" who recently died, the Jehovah's Witnesses, Moonies—Universal Christian Church, or the Mormons).

Still, we are sometimes astonished to hear some of the remarks made regarding such sects, the most current one being, "But they *are* based on the Bible!" It is only one step from this viewpoint to following them. We must encourage all Christians—evangelical, Protestant, Catholic—to read the information and warnings available from those who study the sects.

We freely encourage Christians to work with other evangelical churches whose leaders they know well and whose doctrines they agree with. It is important that the basis of cooperation be clear, otherwise problems will always arise.

A variety of Christian, biblical, and missionary conventions and conferences have proved themselves throughout the years. These have contributed to revival in the churches and to the building up of the faith of believers. Likewise, other newer groups with charismatic or ecumenical orientations draw crowds and revitalize Christians. Everything grows old and changes, and new inspiration does not always come in the same way or at the same place as before.

We are talking here of open, friendly, and biblical collaboration, even though we may not always approve all the positions taken by others. And we readily understand if other evangelical churches refuse to work together with those who do not have the same point of view, the same teachings, the same confession of faith. It is a wise position which helps to avoid many misunderstandings, even though it may appear to be lacking in brotherly spirit.

Collaboration requires mutual respect and unswerving loyalty. A man is loyal to his wife, and vice versa, when he does nothing secretly and acts with integrity toward her. Loyalty to his wife includes loyalty to the wives of others—he will never seek to turn them from their husbands.

It is the same for interchurch relationships. Respect for our own church prevents us from flirting with other churches—loving them in thought more than our own. Respect for the other church leads us to renounce the desire to attract its members to our own group—and especially not under the pretext of bringing them closer to the Lord and to a more real faithfulness to his Word.

c. Questionable Actions

Many Christians are troubled and don't know very well what to believe because of the way they are treated by other believers. For example, is it by the love of God and pure motives that some persons ask other Christians about the condition of their souls and their spiritual experiences? Or is it with the hope (perhaps unadmitted) of enticing them to follow these persons who supposedly have more to offer them than their own congregation does?

The motive of such "outsiders" toward the sick is questionable. This is especially so when the sick are members of an evangelical church which prays for them, visits them, and practices, at their request, the laying on of hands. So often we have seen a "servant of God" come to lay hands on a sick person to perform a healing by any means, without the agreement and cooperation of the sick person's congregation.

At the beginning of the pentecostal movement in France about 30 years ago, I participated in visits at the bedsides of sick persons from my own congregation and others. We prayed or laid on hands for healing. The elders of our churches, influenced by this movement, had taken the initiative for these visits. The results were not always the response the families hoped for, but the process was clear and unambiguous.

At other times I was an invited witness rather than a participant at a healing "performance." I was very ill-at-ease when the leader, with pretended spiritual authority and a crescendoing voice, began to command the sickness and its root of evil to disappear in the name of Christ. This was a confusion of healing with exorcism; it was a debatable action, a source of trouble and disappointment for the families involved, as well as for the congregations. They asked themselves if it was right to act in this way, or if they should rather have followed the biblical pattern of James 5:13-16.

In a small way this is similar to the grand spectacles put on by evangelists who are impelled by a certain religious fanaticism. We sometimes wonder if they are gifted people who are using the church to satisfy an unconscious appetite for power, or if they are truly psychologically and spiritually balanced persons. The Lord can and wants to use the most humble instrument, the despised and the weak, to confound the strong. But alas! These people seem to try to use the Lord rather than allowing the Lord, with his compassion for people, to use them.

Throughout the centuries Christianity has not been exempt from fanaticism. The Inquisition, the Crusades, the affair at Münster during the Reformation are convincing proof. Today we must admit that neither is the part of Christianity called evangelical exempt from seeds of fanaticism. It seems the only explanation for these fanatics and religious quacks is that Satan is controlling them.

3

OTHER CAUSES OF CONFUSION

In the second part of the book we haven't discussed all the things which trouble Christians today in their respective churches. To do so would require too large a book. But even so we must mention briefly two or three other causes of trouble in evangelical churches.

Theology and Theologies

Theology is the "study of God," of the things of God, of divine things, and, by extension, the study of religion. There is no more worthy field of study, no more desirable knowledge, than that of God. But for Christians, the written revelation, the Bible, is the most trustworthy source for this study and knowledge.

"Fundamentalist" theology seems to be the monopoly of the "true evangelicals." Some of them speak of it without really knowing what it's about. On the other hand, "liberalism" or "modernism" in theology is, according to these "true evangelicals," a destructive vice of the mainline churches; in the end, liberalism includes all churches and groups which do not accept exactly as they do the holy Scripture as the word of God.

No. Evangelicals do not have a monopoly on a healthy and respectful attitude toward the Bible. However, sometimes they appear to be saying that the way in which others regard them and the way in which they understand themselves is a criteria of orthodoxy (of the true faith according to the Scriptures).

In this sense we are not fundamentalists in the same way as some others are. For example, some have chosen a certain number of Scriptural truths which are to them fundamental, while they reject as invalid for our age certain other words of the Lord (for example, his words in the Sermon on the Mount). But we are in agreement with them on the divine inspiration and sovereign authority of the Bible in matters of faith and Christian conduct.

These diverse attitudes and different interpretations of the Bible often trouble Christians who aren't used to theological discussions. We can encourage them to humbly submit to the word of God as they understand it, together with the fellow-believers in their church, and to withstand the echoes of some new theology. Yet they should always be open to a better understanding of the holy Scripture in order to better practice its teachings. Teachers and leaders in the local churches, in Bible schools and seminaries—persons known to have the gift of the Spirit and to use it honestly, can lead them in this growth.

This is why qualified teachers are needed in the church. Children, adolescents, and youth are today more than ever subjected to a sort of brainwashing through secular education, and the sometimes anti-Christian orientation of the public schools.

We have seen how various pagan philosophies contaminated or overthrew the faith of the first Christians. What about today? It is important that solid biblical teaching be given in all churches, so that we may recognize those things which assault our senses and minds, our hearts and spirits. The local congregation is the ideal place to deal with these troubles. Here they can be shared and then dissipated—thanks to the sword of the Spirit which is the word of God.

Contradictory Predictions and Prophecies

Churches have split because of different opinions on the Christian future (eschatology). Evangelists and pastors sometimes hold well-defined, but opposing positions on the interpretation of biblical prophecies. Thus, the average Christian can become lost and bewildered.

Let us humbly recognize that we cannot settle by vote the disputes among those who hold opposing views. Because of the self-confident assertions of each group (sometimes accompanied by the condemnation of the other group), they end up strongly opposing rather than strengthening each other. All this upsets and troubles faithful Christians.

Believers already have enough from the world to bother them. It offers them the predictions of so-called seers and futurists. These may be so precise and yet so ambiguous that the gullible can always find a justification for believing them. It reminds me of the 1940s when I was a prisoner of war. The predictions of Nostradamus (a French astrologer and seer of the 16th century) had gained much esteem in the minds of many of the prisoners. They even saw in his predictions the name of General de Gaulle and the announcement of his victory!

Prophecies which seem so clear to some as being fulfilled in present world events appear at the same time very doubtful to others. We want to ask each group not to be too assertive (to be too confident is not in accordance with certain warnings of the Lord). And we ask the others not to let themselves be troubled. They can recognize their uncertainty and be content with it, while actively awaiting the coming of the Lord (1 John 2:28).

I know by experience the disappointment of accepting without question a prediction by one of God's servants concerning the fulfillment of a biblical prophecy only to find it untrue. For example, we can now see that the one who was called "*the* antichrist" in the 1930s and 1940s (Hitler), should have been called "*an* antichrist."

The essential is to be vigilant and faithful, a "wise virgin" who is waiting, not with feverishness but with assurance. We are to have a supply of oil enough for now and always. (The oil is the symbol of the Spirit's anointing, as 1 John 2:26-28 says, "the anointing you received....")

Misuse of the Tongue

We are going to end at the place where we maybe should have begun. The tongue is perhaps the greatest troublemaker. The lives of many Christians are poisoned and the relations among family and church members are deeply disturbed by misuse of the tongue. The apostle James is the one who speaks the most severely of this. But already in Proverbs the tongue's misdeeds are noted. The Lord Jesus also warns us about the dangers of the tongue.

All believers should reread often the third chapter of James and examine how they use their tongue. It's true that Sunday morning during the worship service the tongue is used to praise the Savior, to bless his name, and to sing his praises. At prayer meeting during the week the tongue is used in an even more holy way. But how about when we leave the church and during the times in between our public worship? What then?

The tongues of Christians are often like a cancer in the body. It harms nearby cells, then reaches vital organs. It spreads its sickness, weakening the body, and brings suffering in its slow and sure march toward death.

This cancer may begin with gossip, the words one uses in the joyous recounting of the bad deeds that others have done. How can we talk like this when we know that love covers all faults? The one who is living in Christ by the Holy Spirit will deliberately choose the loving attitude. Too few in our churches do choose the loving way! Alas for those who do not, because according to Proverbs 26:22, "The words of a gossip are like choice morsels; they go down to a man's inmost parts."

Who has never gossiped? Who has never spoken ill of another? It's time for Christians to become conscious of their sin, of the natural inclination they all have to speak evil of their neighbor. "Whoever repeats [an offense] ... separates close friends" (Proverbs 17:9), and sets Christian against Christian! People do not realize that in gossiping they do an enormous wrong to the body of Christ! They think, "It's not so wrong to tell. After all, people need to know...." No! It's a sin. It's the cause of divisions and troubles in the church.

Even more serious are slanderous statements—something bad made up to add to the true or untrue things that have been learned from a talebearer.

Slander is mentioned 15 or 20 times in the Bible. For example: "Do not go about spreading slander among your people" (Leviticus 19:16); "Whoever spreads slander is a fool" (Proverbs 10:18); "Out of the heart come evil thoughts ... slander" (Matthew 15:19)? The many biblical references to slander indicate how serious the problem is.

Sadly, many Christians, claiming to be redeemed, born again, and baptized by the Holy Spirit, surround themselves with an unhealthy atmosphere by their gossip and slander! What a need for repentance! What an obstacle to a real blossoming of their inner life and of the fellowship to which they belong.

One understands why the apostle Paul returns to this point several times: "Get rid of all ... slander, along with every form of malice" (Ephesians 4:31). "You must rid yourselves of all such things as these ... malice, slander, and filthy language" (Colossians 3:8).

These words call us to humble ourselves, recognize our sins in this area, and let ourselves be purified by the Lord through the fire of his Spirit. This is more important than to desire at any cost a certain spiritual gift. To be thus purified is also to be baptized "with the Holy Spirit and with fire" as we were promised (see Matthew 3:11).

Some Advice

We have come to the end of this study. We could doubtless have found other causes of trouble and confusion in the church, such as errors in conduct. Young people readily accuse their elders of being hypocrites, and they're not always wrong. But the youth also offend people, for other reasons. In the happy congregation, members express mutual regard and goodwill, confidence in each other, and enough love and respect to confront together causes of trouble, whatever they may be. Their goal is to find a mutually satisfying solution, with the help of God and for his glory.

One thing is certain. Personal sincerity and thirst for God, even when present in every member of a church, do not prevent trouble. But Christian groups can live the abundant life promised to all who come to Jesus Christ humbly and with faith. The key is to search for a deeper communion with the Lord, experiencing together a more real devotion to God.

The New Testament church was troubled by people and movements which appeared religious but were not solidly founded on the whole word of God. From the examples we noticed among the first churches after Pentecost, we can expect to face a similar reality. Let's ask God for a spirit of discernment and refuse to follow any doubtful "shepherds" from without who seek to impose themselves on us. They do not respect what the Scripture commands concerning spiritual leaders in the local church (see, for example, 1 Thessalonians 5:12, 13; Hebrews 13:7; 1 Peter 5:1-5).

We believe that the invitation, "do not be troubled," goes together with respect for the local pastors and elders. They were chosen according to the will of God by the local church, in faithful submission and obedience. They were chosen to maintain unity among believers, among us. At the time of our baptism, we promised to walk together, watching over each other, encouraging each other in love and good deeds (Hebrews 10:24), while awaiting the return of the Lord (Hebrews 10:25).

EPILOGUE

The author has listed some of the problems faced by the New Testament churches. He also mentions some of the things that confuse Christians today, especially those who live in the Western world.

Perhaps you face different issues within the church where you live. For example, you may confront such things as superstition, witchcraft, worship of ancestors, polygamy, religious rituals, tribalism, nationalism, animism, Eastern religions, and other ideas and practices that distort Christian faith.

Note some of the marks of troublemakers. They may: cling to outdated customs (Acts 15:1); deceive others concerning their authority (Acts 15:24); close themselves to the new work of God's Spirit (Acts 11:15-18); teach false doctrine (Galatians 1:6, 7); allow immoral behavior (Romans 6); promote hollow and deceptive philosophies (Colossians 2:8-10); promote personalities rather than lift up Christ (1 Corinthians 1:10-13); mix pagan practices with biblical truth (Romans 1:24, 25).

Whatever your situation, make good use of the principles shared by the author. These include: basing our faith on the *whole* Word of God; asking God for a spirit of discernment; testing biblical interpretation with spiritual leaders and other sincere Christians (the church); holding fast to the truth as revealed in Christ; living holy lives; trusting Christian brothers and sisters whose faith and love have been proved in both joy and suffering rather than following novices; and confronting false teachers with God's Word.

Perhaps the most important principle is this: to remember that our salvation is based on Christ's life, death, and resurrection. He is the foundation or cornerstone of our redemption; his life and teachings are our model for faith and life. "For no one can lay any foundation other than the one already laid, which is Jesus Christ" (1 Corinthians 3:11).

Much of the confusion within the Christian church often arises over fine points of doctrine or lifestyle rather than basic truths or principles. The teaching of the Scriptures is helpful in facing this problem. For example, in 1 Timothy 1:4 Paul admonishes us *not* to devote ourselves to "myths and endless genealogies. These promote controversies rather than God's work—which is by faith." In Hebrews 12:1, 2 we are encouraged to "throw off everything that hinders and the sin that so easily entangles, and let us run with perseverance the race marked out for us." We are to "fix our eyes on Jesus, the author and perfecter of our faith. . . ."

The gifting of the Spirit mentioned in Ephesians 4 is intended to equip the saints for ministry and to build up the body of Christ so that all may attain unity and maturity in him.

> Then we will no longer be infants, tossed back and forth by the waves, and blown here and there by every wind of teaching and by the cunning and craftiness of men in their deceitful scheming. Instead, speaking the truth in love, we will in all things grow up into him who is the Head, that is, Christ. From him the whole body, joined and held together by every supporting ligament, grows and builds itself up in love, as each part does its work. Ephesians 4:14-16.

The above Scriptures summarize the hope of the gospel. In place of trouble, Christians experience the peace and joy of God that passes all understanding. In Christ we have fullness of life, for he is the head over every power and authority (Colossians 2:10). The birthright of Christians is order, clarity, and purpose, not confusion. May we by faith lay hold of our inheritance in Christ.

—J. Allen Brubaker

FOR FURTHER READING AND STUDY

Drescher, John M. *Spirit Fruit*. Scottdale, Pa.: Herald Press, 1974.

Kuen, Alfred. *Le Saint-Esprit, baptême et plénitude* (The Holy Spirit, Baptism and Fullness). Editions Emmaus, CH 1806 Saint-Légier sur Vevey, Switzerland, 1976.

Maillot, Alphonse. *L'église au présent* (The Church in the Present). Tournon: Editions Réveil, 1978.

Morgan, G. Campbell. *The Spirit of God*. London: Hodder and Stoughton, 1900.

Ranaghan, Kevin and Dorothy. *Catholic Pentecostals*. Paramus, N.J.: Paulist Press, 1969.

Shallis, Ralph. *The Miracle of the Spirit.* Fontenay-sous-Bois: Editions Farel, 1977.

Slaughter, Frank G. *Gospel Fever.* Garden City, N.Y.: Doubleday, 1980.

Wenger, J. C. *Disciples of Jesus.* Scottdale, Pa.: Herald Press, 1977.

_____. *God's Word Written.* Scottdale, Pa.: Herald Press, 1966.

_____. *Introduction to Theology.* Scottdale, Pa.: Herald Press, 1954.

_____. *What Mennonites Believe.* Scottdale, Pa.: Herald Press, 1977.

Pierre Widmer was born in Brognard (Doubs), France, of rural parents, members of the Mennonite congregation in Montbéliard. He received his professional training in the state schools (secondary education in Audincourt, teacher training in Besancon). While teaching public school, he took courses in liberal arts at the university.

Although he received most of his religious training in Mennonite circles, he received further spiritual enrichment from other Christian groups. These were as different from each other as the Lutheran Church and the Salvation Army, and included the Reformed Church, Plymouth Brethren, Baptists, and Pentecostals.

As a prisoner of war from 1939 to 1945 he served as a volunteer Protestant chaplain and during that time was able to continue his general educational and theological studies. His many contacts with persons of widely different background, culture, and conviction strengthened his own biblical, evangelical, and Anabaptist-Mennonite position.

After his return to France he resumed his professional activities as a teacher who loved his work and devoted time to his calling as a Christian leader. He served as an elder of the Montbéliard congregation, as youth leader, as editor of the *Christ Seul* journal, as professor at the Bienenberg Bible School, as one of the co-founders of the Free Evangelical Seminary at Vaux-sur-Seine, and as president of the Mennonite Missions Committee.

He discontinued his public school teaching in 1959 to give himself to a full-time multiple ministry in the Mennonite churches and in relating to churches of other denominations. His broad observation, experience, and pastoral counseling are reflected in this booklet.